Defeating Depression

Lifting Yourself from Sadness into Joy

Dale R. Olen, Ph.D.

D1508875

A Life Skills Series Book

JODA Communications, Ltd.
Milwaukee, Wisconsin

Editor: Carolyn Kott Washburne
Design: Chris Roerden and Associates
Layout: Eileen Olen

ISBN 1-56583-011-3

Published by: JODA Communications, Ltd.
              10125 West North Avenue
              Milwaukee, WI 53226

PRINTED IN THE UNITED STATES OF AMERICA

Table of Contents

Introduction

to the

Life Skills Series

Nobody gets out alive! It isn't easy navigating your way through life. Your relationships, parents, marriage, children, job, school, church, all make big demands on you. Sometimes you feel rather ill-equipped to make this journey. You feel as if you have been tossed out in the cold without even a warm jacket. Life's journey demands considerable skill. Navigating the sometimes smooth, other times treacherous journey calls for a wide variety of tools and talents. When the ride feels like a sailboat pushed by a gentle breeze, slicing through the still waters, you go with the flow. You live naturally with the skills already developed.

But other times (and these other times can make you forget the smooth sailing), the sea turns. The boat shifts violently, driven by the waves' force. At those stormy moments, you look at your personal resources, and they just don't seem sufficient.

Gabriel Marcel, the French philosopher, wrote that the journey of life is like a spiral. The Greeks, he observed, viewed life as *cyclical*—sort of the same old thing over and over. The seasons came, went, and came again. History repeated itself. The Hebrews, on the other hand, saw life as *linear*—a pretty straight march toward a goal. You begin at the Alpha point and end at Omega. It's as simple as that.

Marcel combined the two views by capturing the goal-oriented optimism of the Hebrews and the sobering reality of the Greeks' cycles. Life has its ups and downs, but it always moves forward.

To minimize the *downs* and to make the most of the *ups*, you need **Life Skills**. When you hike down the Grand Canyon, you use particular muscles in your back and legs. And when you trudge up the Canyon, you use other muscles. So too with life skills. You call on certain skills when your life spirals down, such as the skill of defeating depression and managing stress. When your life is on an upswing, you employ skills like thinking reasonably and meeting life head on.

This series of books is about the skills you need for getting through life. To get from beginning to end without falling flat on your face and to achieve some dignity and some self-satisfaction, you need **basic** life skills. These include:

1. Accepting yourself.
2. Thinking reasonably.
3. Meeting life head on.

With these three life skills mastered to some degree, you can get a handle on your life. Now, if you want to build from there, you are going to need a few more skills. These include:

4. Communicating.
5. Managing stress.
6. Being intimate.
7. Resolving conflict.
8. Reducing anger.
9. Overcoming fear.
10. Defeating depression.

If you have these ten skills up and running in your life, you are ready to face yourself, your relationships, your parents, your marriage, your children, your job and even God with the hope of handling whatever comes your way. Without these skills, you are going to bump into one stone wall after another. These skills don't take away the problems, the challenges and the hard times. But they do help you dig out of life's deep trenches and more fully *enjoy* the good times.

Life Skills can be learned. You have what it takes to master each of these skills–even if you feel you don't have the tiniest bit of the skill right now. But nobody can develop the skill for you. You have to take charge and develop it yourself. Your family, friends and community may be able to help you, but you are the center at which each skill has to start. Here is all you need to begin this learning process:

- Awareness.
- The desire to grow.
- Effort and practice.

Awareness begins the process of change. You have to notice yourself, watch your behavior and honestly face your strengths and weaknesses. You have to take stock of each skill and of the obstacles in you that might inhibit its growth.

Once you recognize the value of a skill and focus on it, you have to want to pursue it. The critical principle here, one you will see throughout this series, is *desire*. Your desire will force you to focus on the growing you want to do and keep you going when learning comes hard.

Finally, your *effort and practice* will make these **Life Skills** come alive for you. You can do it. These books are tools to guide and encourage your progress. They are my way of being with you— cheering your efforts. But without your practice, what you find in these books will wash out to sea.

Working on these ten **Life Skills** won't get you through life without any scars. But the effort you put in here will help you measure your life in more than years. Your life will be measured in the zest, faith, love, honesty and generosity you bring to yourself and your relationships.

I can hardly wait for you to get started!

Chapter One

What is Depression?

Depression is the common cold of psychology. You've seen it, felt it, heard it, tasted it and even smelled it. You haven't been able to avoid this one. Perhaps you've called it sadness, melancholy, a mood swing or crabbiness. You've been down, and it hasn't felt good. At times it has snuck in when you weren't expecting it. At other times you knew you were in for a siege of funk.

Most people handle their depressions well. Much of the time you probably do, too. The depression hits. You acknowledge the sadness you feel over some loss, and then you go on to other aspects of your life. The mood lifts, and you feel normal again. But other times the depression overpowers you. It floods your boundaries and settles in with a long lease. With this kind of depression you may need some help, and you need to take some active steps to defeat it.

Depression overwhelms a significant portion of the population. Approximately 75 percent of all psychiatric hospitalizations are due to depression. The power of this psychological condition is so great that many people cannot manage the problem alone. They must enter a hospital for assistance. It has been estimated that 15 percent of all adults in any year suffer significant depressive symptoms. So although 85 percent of the population probably feels depressed at times, they appear to manage quite well. However, any of us may find a life situation or a relationship so difficult that we also might become – or perhaps have already been – part of that 15 percent with significant depression.

Loss is tied to every depression, but depression is not tied to every loss. Most likely you don't get depressed from losing one dollar. But you may get depressed if you have to pay $5,000 more than you expected on your taxes. You probably don't "feel blue" when a neighbor acquaintance moves to another state. But you may well become depressed when your best friend starts a new career in a foreign country. You certainly don't feel depressed if you lose that 10 pounds you could never get off before. But you would most definitely depress yourself if you lost both your legs in a car accident.

To become depressed, the loss you experience must be significant. When you lose a dollar – or $10 – you may get angry with yourself, but you probably don't get depressed because it isn't that big a deal. Small losses feel more annoying than saddening. You can't find your keys when you want them. You don't know where you put that telephone number. Your son used the wrench and didn't put it back. Now you can't find it and are angry with him. These aren't the losses of depression.

Depression occurs when you lose those things that are most important and valuable to you. Usually that means relationships, career, the means of providing for others and self, and any loss of self-worth.

Jack was in the midst of a divorce. He initiated it because the marriage had not been working for several years. His three children were still under 10 years old, and he knew his wife would get custody. He also knew that supporting two dwellings would create havoc in his financial life. He wouldn't be able to give his kids the life style he dreamed of for them.

Although Jack felt relief that he was ending his marriage, he became more and more depressed as the process went on. He realized he was losing his children. His relationship with them would be forever altered. He feared they would drift further and further from him as they got older. Furthermore, he saw his goal of financial security and independence sliding further from reality. He wanted to create a fund for his children's college education and hoped to retire by age 55 with a condo in Florida. No way could he do that now. The loss of his dream of providing for his children and gaining early retirement led to further depression.

Along with significant loss, another ingredient is necessary for depression to overwhelm you. You must also feel unable to retrieve what is lost or to substitute something for it. No longer will Jack have the same kind of relationship with his children. No longer will he have the type of marriage with Debbie he once had or wished he could have had. Jack lost significant aspects of his domain, *and* he felt the losses were permanent. He would never regain what had been lost.

On the day Jack moved out of the home and into his sterile apartment, he realized what he was losing. That was a sad moment for him. But his depression ballooned when he further realized the negative effect of his loss on his *future.*

Most losses feel significant insofar as they negatively affect your future. If they don't influence the rest of your life, you may feel some sadness over the present loss, but you don't remain depressed. Sports serves the best example of this. You root hard for the home team. They get to the championship game. They lose by a point. You feel awful. But within an hour or a day you're over the loss and on with your life. Why? Because that loss does not have any negative effect on your future.

On the other hand, if your husband or wife dies, you become depressed not only for the immediate loss, but because you realize the negative effect of that loss on your future. Often people complain of depression months *after* a death. They say they felt sad at the time of death, but it seems worse later on. The depression sets in because later on they realize the impact of their spouse's death on their future. They say, "He will never return. It won't ever be the same. I now have to do all these things by myself."

Depression, then, involves three aspects:

1. The significant loss of something or someone valuable to you.
2. The inability to retrieve or substitute for the loss.
3. The realization of the negative effects the loss has on your future.

Depression happens when you lose something significant *and* think about it in negative ways.

Like most people you may believe depression happens *to you.* Your house gets blown away in a tornado and you get depressed. Bad things do happen to good people, to paraphrase a popular self-help book. But *your interaction* with the bad things that happen out there is what really causes the depression. If you live your life with few positive interactions with the outside world, you will probably grow up being depressed. If you experience normal positive interactions with your world, you will develop into a happy, at-peace person.

If you grow up in an environment filled with conflict instead of love, in an environment of emotional or physical abuse, your chances for depression are obviously greater than if you grow up in a loving, peaceful environment. Such a negative world teaches you to think in negative, pessimistic ways. Thinking in such dark ways leads you to interpret future life events in an equally bleak manner. Negative experiences feed upon themselves, creating pessimistic thinking, which in turn creates a more negative view of the world.

But certain people who grow up in this negative cycle have been able to change it. They have done something within themselves to stop the cycle. One woman, Jenny, raised in a home devoid of love and warmth, grew up to become a happy, loving wife, mother and career woman. She interacted with very negative circumstances for the first 14 years of her life. Fortunately for her, she went off to a boarding convent school where the sisters supplied her with the love and warmth she never received at home. She grew into a sensitive, delightful person whose optimism and spontaneity continue to be contagious and life-giving.

Even if you have experienced the dark side of life, you can respond in non-depressive ways. Depression needs both you *and* your outer world. The outside world, at times, can be quite cruel. But your inner attitudes and approach to it can do much to offset the harshness the world sometimes presents. This will be discussed more fully in the section on "Principles and Tools for Defeating Depression."

Depression affects four aspects of your life: motivation, thoughts, self-esteem and emotions.

When you're depressed, you don't feel like doing much. *Motivation* leaves you because your loss takes with it meaning and purpose. Without a purpose you cannot take action. If you lose out on a promotion to another employee, you may no longer feel like working at the same company. Your motivation vanishes. If your husband or wife dies suddenly and your kids are all grown and gone, you will experience a dramatic drop in motivation. There is little purpose to go on, especially if you have been working to prepare for retirement with your partner.

Oftentimes people make the mistake of getting upset with a depressed person because "he just sits there doing nothing." For instance, when a man gets laid off from his job of 18 years, he experiences depression. He comes home and sits, unable to do anything. His wife, who feels badly for him, treats him kindly for a while. But the longer he sits, the more anxious she becomes. Her anxiety turns to irritation, and she begins pushing him to get going. The more she pushes, the more depressed he becomes. And the more depressed he gets, the less motivation he has. Remember, decreased motivation goes along with increased depression.

While your thoughts help create your depression, your depression also creates *negative thoughts*. Herein lies the vicious cycle of depression. You think your situation in life won't get any better. So you feel depressed. The more depressed you feel about your future, the more you view it negatively. Of course, if your future is without redemption, why try? Thus, your negative thoughts cause you to lose motivation. Throughout this book I will talk with you about the power of your thoughts in overcoming depression. But here I want you to understand that depression darkly colors your thoughts as well.

When a major loss hits you, you also lose your sense of purpose and direction. Once you view your life as without meaning, then it's an easy step to conclude, "Therefore, I must be useless or worthless." Now you have tapped into the deepest loss of all – the *loss of self*. At the very core of depression, self-esteem is eaten up. The original loss to you is most likely something external. But if that loss is fed and nurtured by your negative thinking, it eventually plays havoc with your self-esteem. You cannot easily sustain a positive view of yourself while suffering from depression.

Finally, depression tends to zap all of your *emotions*. In a state of depression you don't feel much else. For example, people who experience the death of a loved one often report feeling "numb." They have no feeling. They really do, of course. It's the feeling of depression. But they sense little else.

Depression mutes your other feelings. It takes too much energy to get angry or jealous or happy. If you're depressed, you certainly don't feel calm or content or peaceful. You might feel some anxiety or fear, but those feelings also are minimized. Depressed people don't care about the dangers around them, so their fear remains low.

Depression, then, has a powerful impact on you. Others may tell you to pull yourself out of your depression. They may insist that you use more "will power" to get yourself going. Easy for them to say, right? Depression doesn't just go away because you will it to do so. It does take hard work, of course. And it helps to have some support from your friends or family. Your hard work, your will power and the support of people who care for you are what's needed to overcome depression and all its painful effects.

Depression has many symptoms.

Although you know the feeling of depression, I'd like you to understand the signs of depression. There are many. You don't need all of these to conclude you must be depressed. On the other hand, if you only have one or two of these symptoms, you are not necessarily depressed, either. Here they are in no particular order of importance:

Negative thoughts and expressions about yourself.

Dejected mood.

Thoughts of suicide.

Feelings of hopelessness, pessimistic thoughts.

Feelings of inadequacy or helplessness.

Difficulty in making decisions.

Loss of interests and enjoyment.

Feelings of guilt.

Loss of motivation.

Loss of sexual drive.

Withdrawal from others.

Crying spells.

Loss of or increased appetite.

Sleep disturbance.

Fatigue.

Constipation.

Slowed down thoughts.

Decrease in physical activity.

If you show several of these signs, you are most likely experiencing depression. If these signs continue for some time, then you can be pretty sure you are depressed. If these symptoms persist, you do yourself a service by consulting a psychologist or mental health professional as well as your personal physician.

Chapter Two

Types of Depression

O ver the years psychologists have attempted to classify depression. While a hundred varieties can be abstracted and defined, for our purposes just a few distinctions are needed. Depression can be *external* or *internal* in its cause. It can be *psychological* and/or *biochemical* in origin. It can also be considered *mild* or *severe*.

External depression begins from an outside loss.

This type of depression, sometimes referred to as the "garden variety," happens to everyone. As indicated above, whenever you experience a significant loss and have little power to reverse it, you know external depression. It usually demands some personal work and passes in time.

The most common form of this depression is *grief.* You usually reserve grief for the most significant and meaningful losses in your life. The death of a loved one tops the list. But there are other losses as well that need to be grieved, such as the loss of bodily functioning, as occurs in accidents resulting in paralysis; the loss of a long-standing and satisfying career; the displacement of friends and family; children leaving home; and the loss of significant love in your childhood through the experience of physical, sexual or emotional abuse.

Psychiatrist and author Elizabeth Kubler-Ross clarified the "process of grief." She helped us understand that people go through various "steps" in the grieving process. In her classic description, grief followed these five stages:

1. *Denial*: The individual does not accept the loss as having happened.
2. *Negotiation*: The person makes promises and commitments to win back what was lost. "If you return to me, I'll never drink again."
3. *Depression*: The person experiences sadness due to the loss.
4. *Anger*: The person looks for an external cause of her loss, blames it and becomes angry with it. Often, the anger is directed to the one who left.
5. *Acceptance*: Finally, the person integrates the loss with her reality. Although it still hurts, she learns to say "yes" to it and moves on in her own life without the other.

Grief work is precisely that–work. It demands much of you. You cannot avoid it, since you will or have experienced important losses in your life. The depth of pain and sadness you feel at these times is normal. Your grief should subside with time and with your work of facing and accepting the loss.

The pain of a loved one's death never completely leaves you. But the deep grief and sadness will. The pain that touches you the rest of your life when you think of the one who died serves as a signal to you of your love for that person. The pain remains because your love remains. Celebrating your love helps you soothe the grief.

Internal depression tends to be stable, long-term and low-grade.

This type of depression is tough. It's ingrained. It's been practiced, often for years. It starts early and is part and parcel of a person's life. She knows no other experience. When you ask this person what she has lost, she isn't able to identify anything. With external depression, the individual almost always knows what she has lost and therefore what is causing the depression.

In this case, you have an overall negative feeling about yourself. Self-esteem is usually low. You tend to see the world pessimistically. Negative thinking dominates your thought processes. You experience fatigue and lethargy. Doesn't sound good, does it? All of these symptoms, however, stem from the one – poor self-concept. Thus, the hard work that needs to be done with this type of depression circles around the issue of self-worth. (For more on this subject, read the **Life Skills Series** book *Accepting Yourself.*)

Some depression may be biological in origin.

More and more evidence appears indicating a biological basis for some depressions. We still don't have accurate diagnostic tools to tell which depressions are biological in origin and which are psychological. Trial and error seems to be the most common way used by mental health professionals to determine the cause.

Through an in-depth interview some good guesses at the origin of depression can be made. For example, if the client cannot find any significant losses in his life yet experiences depressive attacks that overwhelm him, the depression may well be biological in origin. This is different from internally created, low-grade depression, because these depressive episodes really interfere in the person's life. They knock him out for a while.

Furthermore, if a person comes from a family where significant depression occurred, it could signal a biological cause of the depression. In particular, if there is any history of bi-polar depression in the family, a biological factor can be influencing the present mood. Bi-polar depression causes an emotional roller-coaster. One moment a person can be extremely depressed, and the next moment he can be euphoric, highly energized and agitated. This is referred to as being "manic." Bi-polar depression responds quite well to certain medications, in particular to lithium.

If there are sufficient indications that the depression has a biological base, then a psychiatrist prescribes an anti-depressant medication. Usually the medication should take full effect within a couple of weeks. To fit the person, the medication may have to be adjusted up or down or changed to a different type. If the medication works, then the psychiatrist tends to conclude the depression is based on biological causes. If the medication doesn't work, the doctor may think the cause is psychological.

Sometimes people take anti-depressant medication temporarily while in the midst of a major depressive period. They need something to help stop the downward spiral quickly. Once they work through their depression and return to a happier state, they can let go of the medication.

Other times individuals may have to remain on medication for long periods, sometimes for the rest of their lives, because the depression is clearly biologically based. Then they need to view taking such medication as they would any other medicine that makes up for a deficiency in their systems. A perfect example of such a medication is "thyroxin." Often women's thyroid glands break down, especially after having children. Thyroxin must be taken daily to substitute for the thyroid that isn't functioning fully. No big deal. The same may be true for some people who need an anti-depressant medication to help the chemical balance of their bodies. Although many people resist the idea of taking anti-depressant medication, the fact is that it supplies the body with elements it lacks. Without those elements, the depression continues.

No matter how biological a depression may be, it always has psychological aspects to it. Just taking medication for depression does not generally defeat it. Medication may alleviate some of the symptoms, but you must work also on your thoughts and psychological processes. You still need the tools and skills described later in this book to reduce and eliminate your depression.

Depression can be mild or severe.

This distinction makes immediate sense to you. Like most other psychological phenomena, it has *degrees* of seriousness. In mild depression the depressed feelings quickly leave you. You simply have a "bad day" or a "bad week." You also don't want the despondent feeling, and you still have enough energy to act against it. Finally, while you might even have suicidal thoughts at times, you make conscious choices not to act on those thoughts.

In more severe depression the sad mood persists and often increases. Feelings of total helplessness and loss of control over your life pervade you. You lose hope as well. When the depression is severe, you may attempt suicide. Finally, your thinking processes become distorted. You may have difficulty making reasonable decisions or even difficulty making any decisions at all. The spinning cycle of depression is like a rip tide that draws you deeper and deeper into a sea of darkness.

Some depressions you can handle alone. Others need help from the outside. If your depression is mild and externally caused, you can assume it's a normal dip in life. By thinking positively and getting on with your daily activities, you can usually overcome these kinds of depression without professional assistance.

But if the depression controls you and becomes more and more severe, you need to seek professional help. Also, if the depression has been long-standing and seems to come from within you (no external losses to speak of), then you will most likely benefit from professional help as well. Don't let yourself think, "Oh, I don't need to go to counseling. I'm not crazy. The counselor will think my problem is so small." That's not true. All of us who counsel recognize the seriousness of depression and the impact that it has on people's lives. By seeking help with your depression, you take a significant step toward moving to a happier, more positive state.

Chapter Three

Causes of Depression

When you become depressed, it certainly seems to be caused by something outside of you, right? Yet psychologists continue to say – and I among them – that *you* cause your own depression. I believe that the way you think and respond to a situation of loss determines your mood. You don't have control over every loss that takes place in your life; but you do always have control over your thoughts and reactions to those losses. The skill of defeating depression lies within you.

Specific thoughts lead directly to depression.

I can guarantee you will become depressed if you routinely think the following thoughts:

Negative thoughts

You give power to what you focus on. This important principle in mental health applies most significantly to depression. Every positive reality possesses a negative thread, just as every negative reality contains a positive element. Depressive people pay attention to the negative threads. By giving so much power to the negative aspects of a situation, these people generate their own depression.

Self-condemning thoughts

You depress yourself when you're very intolerant of your own behavior. With self-condemning thoughts you beat yourself up for not performing perfectly. If you make a mistake, you can't let it go. You have to keep rubbing your nose in it.

All-or-nothing thoughts

Success equals absolute perfection. Anything short of that perfection equals failure. Now, that kind of thinking gets you depressed in a hurry. Why? Because in this life, it's pretty hard to consistently get to "absolute perfection."

All-or-nothing thinking doesn't allow for any grays in a world made up of shades of black and white with colors galore in between. To accept those shades for everyone else but not for yourself guarantees depression.

Causal thoughts

When you think that your successes are caused by external forces while your failures are your own fault, you flirt with depression. You never get rewarded with this kind of thinking. You become your own worst enemy. You can't win with the premise that anything good happening to you must be due to someone or something outside of you, and anything bad that happens must be your fault. So you make a great meal and say it was easy. You just followed directions. You make a good golf shot and think it was luck. You negotiate a new contract and claim the customer was cooperative.

On the other hand, the souffle flops and you conclude you're a bad cook. You hit the golf ball into the water and say you never could get this game right. You lose a sale and decide you're not cut out to be a salesperson. You get angry with the kids and feel like a failure as a parent. Your mother-in-law snaps at you and you moan what a lousy relative you are.

Helpless thoughts

Depression has hooks within it that grab you and pull you further down. Becoming helpless is one of the worst hooks. Because you sense forces out of your control taking something you value, you feel powerless to act against them. You often feel trapped and unable to respond to the situation. If you believe you can't get back what you lost, then you stop looking for it. Your actions slow down. If you feel powerless, you lose motivation to act. Even your thinking process slows down. It seems to take too much energy to focus, problem solve and think through your circumstances.

Imagine that you have been rejected by a man with whom you had an intense and intimate relationship. You try to get him back but without success. The less he responds to your calls and letters, the more helpless you begin to feel. When you reach the state of complete helplessness, when you know your efforts will not win him back, you feel the depth of depression. At that time you also know what it means to be without power.

If you are a master of learned helplessness, you conclude about yourself: "It was my fault he left me. I simply can't relate to men. I will never have a satisfying relationship with a man." Accepting this conclusion, you now feel helpless regarding any future relationship with a man. If you believe you can't do it, then you give up and don't try. Your motivation slows down. Your social interactions dry up, at least with men.

Feeling helpless makes you feel like a victim. In the state of depression, you actually see yourself as a victim of your own mood. In the midst of depression it's very difficult to see your own thoughts and reactions as the *cause* of the depression. You automatically feel victimized. Consequently, you immediately lose the power to overcome the depression itself. You take a *passive* stance toward the depression, thus feeding it. So the depression rises in you because of a triggering event, plus the way you think and react to the event. When the waves of depression begin overwhelming you, you feel as though you cannot stop them. That feeling of helplessness causes you to sink further and further into the depression. Since you don't think you caused the depression and since it feels so overwhelming, you give up and let it engulf you.

As you will see in the next chapter, one of the best challenges to depression is to *actively fight* it. In dealing with depression, you never want to give up your own power. When you do give up your power, depression carries you to ever-deeper and more painful levels.

Depression can occur when you continually seek immediate rewards rather than more significant rewards later on.

While your erroneous thinking stands as the first cause of depression, your behavior and your reactions to triggering events of loss become your second cause of depression. Your behavior – or lack of it – can spin you down into a darker hole and a more trapped spot. Seeking immediate gratification is one of the more common and powerful behaviors that leads to depression.

What do I mean? You're trying to lose weight. You don't like how you look with that extra ten pounds. But you walk into the kitchen on a Saturday afternoon and find the cookie jar. You ingest every cookie there. That's the immediate gratification. They taste great while you're eating them. But later you begin feeling down. You realize you acted against your goal. The next morning you step on the scale and it shows a one-pound gain. You feel depressed.

Certainly you won't depress yours every time you satisfy an

immediate pleasure that interferes with a greater, later pleasure. You can decide to watch a television program instead of finishing that report since you still have two weeks before it's due. But depression becomes an issue if you make it a pattern in your life to take the present pleasure and suffer the loss of the later pleasure.

If you're a spender instead of a saver, you know what I mean about satisfying present pleasures and losing out on later pleasures. You get money, see something you like and buy it. You do this so regularly that you never have any money saved up. Along comes an opportunity to take a European trip with some friends, but you must decline the offer because you have no money. You feel sad and frustrated that you can't go. Now you wish you had saved some money.

Immediate verses delayed gratification shows up mostly in *procrastination* and *withdrawal*. As a normal human being you're going to procrastinate some of the time. But if you make it a habit, it tends to feed an already existing depression or helps to create a low-grade steady depression. When you procrastinate, you always decide on an immediate pleasure over some delayed pleasure. Often your decision not to do something is based on not having the energy to do it at the present time. It's easier to just sit. You should change the light bulb in the bathroom right now, but it's too hard to walk down to the basement where you keep the extra bulbs.

Procrastinating forces you to carry the burdens of all you still have to do. Physically you would feel weighted down if an extra 50 pounds were strapped to your back and you carried it everywhere you went. The same happens psychologically when you procrastinate regularly. You still have to do everything on your to-do list. All those obligations sit on your shoulders like heavy weights. That heaviness is depression.

Withdrawal can also cause depression. You decide you'd rather sit home instead of getting dressed up and interacting with people at the party. Again, all of us feel that way at times. There are gatherings we'd simply rather not attend. But if you make such withdrawal a regular pattern, you begin isolating yourself and find yourself doing less and less with other people. Depression feeds itself when you're alone. It gives you too much time to use your negative thinking. Without people around, you don't need to act. You don't do anything, which results in further depression because you feel so useless.

When you withdraw or procrastinate, it feels immediately better than the alternative of getting out there, taking action, fixing your child's bike or weeding the garden. Obviously, then, one of the best ways of breaking depression is to engage your life, get into action and don't delay doing what needs doing. On the other hand, maintaining discipline in your life is also important. You need to resist the temptations of immediate gratification if the trade-off results in greater depression.

You can create depression as a way of taking care of yourself when no one else is doing so.

I know this may sound backward and confusing. But let me explain. If you are always "giving" to others, focused on their good, you will eventually feel emptied out. You need to be filled up. But what if no one is doing that for you. Then you must do it yourself. One unfortunate way you can do this is by depressing yourself. Really.

Depression turns your focus away from others and onto yourself. It redirects your attention away from giving to others and toward receiving for yourself. When you think about it, physical illness does the same. If you feel nauseated, it's hard to extend yourself to others in a helping way. You just want to go to bed, be alone and moan. Or if you have a headache, it can be very difficult for you to listen attentively to your friend unload the burdens of her day to you. Physical or mental distress re-orients you inward, toward taking care of yourself.

This dynamic is often used by people in care-giving occupations.

Mothers, psychologists, physicians, therapists, nurses, social work-
ers and so on experience this occupational hazard of depressing
themselves as a way of nurturing themselves. It doesn't work very
well, but they still do it anyway.

It works like this: Ann is a social worker, employed by the local
school district. Her case load is so intense that she never takes a break
except for a 15-minute lunch, usually while reviewing a student
report. She never finishes her work and tends to stay after regular
hours, but she can't stay too long because her own children have
already been home from school alone for an hour. So she rushes
home, attends to their needs and immediately begins preparing
supper. Her husband comes home at six o'clock. They eat and
immediately clean the kitchen. She gets a load of wash in while he
vacuums the front room. She then spends some time with her son on
his homework, reads a book with her daughter, helps them get ready
for bed and goes to bed herself.

Ann has been in a giving mode for 18 hours of the day. The other
six hours she has been sleeping. No one has filled her up with love,
attention or praise. No one has given her a moment of relief, lifted any
burdens from her. She has poured herself out but now she needs to
be filled up. Unfortunately, there is no way she can get filled up. So
she begins feeling depressed. This depression works as a survival
mechanism, forcing her to turn toward herself. But turning toward
herself through depression is far from productive. It ends up driving
her further down. Nonetheless at least she can feel sorry for herself,
let herself realize how difficult her life is and how no one seems to
care. In her depression she soothes herself.

In a way, depressing herself at this time is like giving herself a
back rub. You know how hard it would be to give yourself a back rub.
It wouldn't really work, would it? You'd get frustrated, feel unsat-
isfied and quit. Well, Ann depressing herself in this way ends in
similar frustration. It's her effort to give herself a psychological back
rub. It's a way of trying to take care of herself, but it doesn't work.

Depression, then, turns you toward yourself, but it doesn't fill you up. If you experience this type of depression, then use it only as a sign that you're running on empty and need to get some filling up. Make a choice not to use depression as the way to do it. Turn immediately to someone, explain what's happening and ask for what you need. Get your filling up from other people or leisure activities, not from your own depression.

As you can see, the causes of depression are many. However, they all funnel in to *you*. You create those depressions that are sustained and deep. Certainly there are triggering events that cause the losses in your life. But everybody has those. If you remain depressed over those losses, it's because your thinking and behavioral responses are keeping the depression alive. I say this not as a way of blaming you for depression but as a way of helping you understand that you have power over your depression. If your depression happens *to* you, then you are powerless. You are its victim. But if *you* create your depression by the way you think and react, then you have the power to overcome your depression.

Now let's talk about the tools you have at your disposal to overcome depression.

Chapter Four

Principles and Tools for Defeating Depression

You are the tool to defeat depression. From here on all the ways I discuss to overcome depression stem from you. The essential awareness you need is that depression happens inside of you. It happens because of the way you *think* and because you fail to *take action* when you feel depressed. You are not the victim of your depression. You are its creator and its master. You can also become its slayer.

Principle 1

Recognize and challenge depressive beliefs in a systematic way.

When you depress yourself, you make it particularly difficult to problem solve. Unfortunately, your biggest problem at the time is precisely your depression. So you're already in a big hole – you have a problem, namely your depression, but because you're depressed, you have trouble solving the problem of depression. Furthermore, you don't feel like working on it anyway. It seems too hard.

Given this set of spiraling dynamics, you need to put structure and discipline into your efforts to defeat your depression. Writing things down helps you structure these efforts. It also prompts you to higher levels of awareness about your depressive beliefs.

The writing method I like involves an approach called the "ABCs of emotions." It was developed years ago by Albert Ellis, Ph.D., an advocate of cognitive therapy. You will find me using this model in other books in this series as well.

> *A* - stands for *Activating Event*. In this case, the experience of loss.
>
> *B* - stands for your *Beliefs* about the loss.
>
> *C* - stands for the *Consequences* you experience after A and B. You have emotional and behavioral reactions. This is where you feel the depression.
>
> *D* - stands for *Disputing* your depressive beliefs. This is where you take charge of your beliefs and change them.
>
> *E* - stands for the *Effect* on you of changing your beliefs to more positive and realistic ways of seeing yourself and your world.

Here's how this writing method works:

Sandy lived in a "trapped marriage." She was married 17 years and had three children, ages 16, 13 and 8. Over the years, she and her husband drifted apart. There was no love left in the marriage. She felt alone in it, unsupported and unappreciated. She wanted out. But she couldn't leave because of the kids and the finances. She had no career of her own and didn't know how she would support herself and her children. So she depressed herself with her thoughts of helplessness.

Her job was to get free from the depression that was sapping her energy. She was to write out her ABC's. Here's what she wrote, with a little help from her therapist.

ABCs of my depression

A. *Activating event:*

I realize how lousy my marriage is and that it probably isn't going to change. The loss I experience is my dream of having a close loving family.

B. *My beliefs:*

1. This is the worst thing that could ever happen to me.
2. I am a failure, and everyone will look down on me if I am a "divorcee."
3. I am incapable and inadequate when it comes to giving love to another person.
4. I will never find a satisfying relationship for the rest of my life.
5. I see no way out of this mess. I would like to go to sleep and never wake up.
6. I have spent all these years trying to reach my goal of a close-knit family, and I have failed. All this time has been wasted.

C. *The consequences:*

I am very depressed and at times suicidal. I feel trapped with no way out. I feel powerless to change my situation.

D. *Dispute my beliefs:*

1. Wait a minute. There are worse things that could hapen. I still have my children. They are a delight to me. I have my health, and I have my friends. I just don't have a husband.
2. I am not a failure because my marriage has ended. There are many causes for the break-up of this marriage.

Certainly I must take responsibility for being part of this relationship ending, but it doesn't mean it was all my fault. Given both of our family backgrounds, it isn't surprising that our marriage is grinding to a halt. Also, people today are used to divorce. They may be surprised at first when I announce I'm divorced. But my good friends will understand and remain supportive. And those that don't know me well won't spend much time thinking or judging me anyway. I'm not that important to them.

3. Although I question my ability to love another person well, I know I have great love for my children. I also know I have good friends and feel close and loving toward them. I love my brother, who is a man. So even if I no longer love my husband, it doesn't mean I am incapable of loving a man. I just don't love *this* man anymore.

4. I can't predict how my life will look in the future. Right now it seems as though I will never find another man. In fact, at this point, that doesn't even seem appealing. So I'm going to make the decision *not* to enter another relationship. I could if I wanted to, but I am choosing not to at this time. I will live in the present moment with my choice and not focus on the future.

5. I choose not to think in suicidal terms. I realize the only reason I even have such thoughts is because I feel trapped. For now I consciously choose life in this situation rather than ending it by killing myself.

6. The past 17 years have brought a number of very good things. Certainly my children. I wouldn't have these particular, wonderful kids had I not married Jim. We have also had many good times over the years. I have grown as a person, I think. In fact, the reason I have considered divorce is precisely because I have grown so much in the last seven or eight years. Thinking about divorce is

actually a sign of how far I have come!

E. *Effects of disputing*:

I couldn't feel much change right away. I didn't believe my "disputes." I wasn't very convincing. But as I thought about my disputes more, I became more convinced. Now I'm feeling stronger and in control of my life. I don't feel so trapped and certainly feel less depressed. I still have a ways to go, but I sense I'm at least on the road.

Sandy took this writing task seriously. She spent time thinking about her thinking. She didn't write all her beliefs down at one sitting. It took several days to get those thoughts on paper. When a thought popped into her mind, she wrote it down right away. That way she didn't forget it. When she disputed her depressive thoughts, she did sit down and take some time. At first, she reported, the disputing part was difficult. She couldn't think of any challenging thoughts. But as she stayed with it, she began thinking in more challenging ways.

You can appreciate the discipline Sandy needed to accomplish this task. But the results were worth it to her. She took charge of her thoughts and, therefore, of her depression.

Another structured way to defeat depression involves creating a hypothesis and testing it out. Sandy was instructed to take one of her depressive beliefs, form a challenge to it and *test it* out. Here's what she did.

She took the depressive belief that "Everyone will look down on me if I am divorced." Her challenging hypothesis was: "Those who love me will still love me even if I'm divorced. And those who are only acquaintances will not care much either way." Now she had to test the hypothesis.

In general she didn't want to tell people she was thinking of getting divorced. Nor did she want to know what others thought about her decision. She felt comfortable, however, with asking her two closest friends. So she questioned them directly about how they would react to her if she decided to divorce her husband. They both responded in very supportive ways, stating they sensed such a decision was in the wind.

In checking out reactions with other people, Sandy needed to be more indirect. So she tried to engage her acquaintances in conversations about divorced people they both knew. She was looking for hints about their level of acceptance. Generally she found these people very tolerant and matter-of-fact about other people's divorces. She also tried to find out if their relationship to the "divorced one" had changed in any way. Again, she found people were still on friendly terms with the divorced person. The only exception was in those situations were the *couples* had been friends. In some situations the friendships had simply ended.

By creating hypotheses against your depressive beliefs and by testing them out, you add much more weight to your new, more positive and realistic ways of thinking. You're also taking action, which in itself begins your fight against depression. So make yourself *work* at overcoming your depression. Thinking, writing and checking out your new thoughts through new behaviors are essential ingredients in defeating depression.

Principle 2

Learn to focus on and appreciate the positive, life-giving aspects of your world.

Remember, you give power to what you focus on. By paying attention to the positive events in your life, you gradually give them power. To make the shift from negative thinking to positive thinking, you need discipline. Assume your negative thinking is your *addiction.* You have to break the addiction the same way alcoholics break theirs. You use *force* and you do it *one day or hour at a time.* You know your negative thinking causes your depression. Focus on your goal of defeating depression by fighting those negative thoughts. You don't always have to replace them. You need only to *notice* the positives that take place in your life.

Positive and neutral events outpace negative events in your life. However, when you feel depressed, you don't realize there are any positive aspects in your world. Your negative focus dominates your psychic screen. So you need to create ways of *paying attention to the positives*. One way of doing this is to keep track of pleasant and unpleasant events.

Years ago I did a piece of research on the factors influencing commitment to a cause. I had people keep a record of all the settings they entered during a two week period. They wrote down the setting, what they did in it and who else was there. They also indicated if they experienced the event as positive, negative or neutral.

After tabulating the results, I discovered a happy sidelight. Everybody had many more positive and neutral experiences than negative ones. And some of those people were depressed during the two week period. While some difficult situations triggered their depression, it was clear that their focusing on the negatives kept the depression going. They missed the positives, eventhough they recorded more positive and neutral events than negative events.

One of your first activities, then, when you feel depressed, is to realize that you're blocking out your awareness and appreciation of positive events. So try hard to look for them. Pay attention to *all* that happens in your daily life. Much of it is positive. Even if the event seems trivial, it will tend to lift your mood. Your mood is related to activity, both positive and negative. If your activity is perceived by you as negative, your mood is down. If you see your activity as positive, your mood rises. To overcome depression, you need to understand the basic relationship between your mood and your perception of daily happenings.

Seeing and saying "yes" to positive events or actions tends to lift your mood. Notice how your daughter cooperated with you in setting the dinner table. Be aware that your husband gave you a kiss, asked how your day was and even listened to your answer. Pay attention to the fact that you enjoyed watching your favorite television show tonight. Celebrate the fact that your car worked fine, your dog did his duty outside, the sun shone for much of the day and you received no bills in the mail. You finally wrote that belated birthday card to your friend in Tennessee. You got three loads of wash done today and pretty well caught up on the laundry. Nobody complained about what you cooked for supper.

Look for the obvious, because much of it is positive. The negative stands out only because there isn't so much of it. When the negative does come, you notice it more quickly.

Principle 3

See your successes in *degrees*, not only in the perfect accomplishment.

Phil was fast approaching the end of his marriage. After 26 years he and his wife were going through a divorce. He was depressed. He had failed as a husband and a father. He had not kept the family together. Even though his children were grown and out of the house, he condemned himself as an inadequate father *now* because the family wouldn't know where to come and what to do during holidays. They wouldn't be together and happy. His sense of failure was complete. He berated himself, claiming he should never have gotten married in the first place. He had damaged the children irreparably.

This, of course, is a classic example of the "all-or-nothing thinking" that I mentioned earlier as a cause of depression. On a scale of one to ten, Phil believed he was a one – a total failure as a parent.

Phil's Parenting

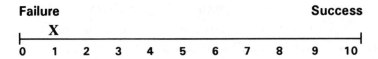

Failure   **Success**

X

0   1   2   3   4   5   6   7   8   9   10

The fight to overcome depression involves getting that "X" to move up the scale toward a sense of success. Phil believed that if he didn't parent perfectly, he had therefore failed. To challenge that thinking, he needed to realize success has *degrees*. In fact, he spent a lot of time with his children when they were young, at a time when many fathers didn't spend much time with their children. He played with them; he did homework with them; he coached their teams; he took them on camping trips; he drove them to friends' houses; he attended parent-teacher conferences.

The one thing he didn't do was keep the family together after everyone grew up. Christmas, Easter, weddings, funerals and other special occasions wouldn't be the same any longer. That made him sad. But it didn't make him a failure as a father.

Phil's Parenting

Failure   **Success**

X

0   1   2   3   4   5   6   7   8   9   10

Measuring by degrees of success, Phil did very well. He didn't hit the final mark as he wanted to, but he certainly did many of the fatherly things that helped his children grow to be well-functioning adults.

If you think like Phil did, you need to challenge your all-or-nothing thinking. When you hear that deadly voice inside pushing you back on the scale to "1"– total failure, total jerk, total incompetent – then you need to fight. Insist you are further up on the scale. There are not only two judgments to be made: Total success or total failure. There are degrees of success. You're on the scale toward success. Remind yourself of baseball players who are considered very successful if they get three hits every ten times they come to bat. And major businesses consider it average to have one successful product marketed for every twenty they try out. That's not a very good success rate. Such companies must be complete failures. No, they just keep on trying until they hit the one successful product. Some companies even celebrate the failures, because the failures bring them one step closer to their next success. Now that's a healthy way of looking at yourself.

Principle 4

Learn to take credit for your successes.

Depressed people tend to blame themselves when things go wrong. And they give credit to others, to fate or to the stars when things go right. Your challenge, when depressed, is to turn that thinking completely around.

Start with compliments. Instead of disclaiming them or pointing out the unsuccessful aspects of what you did, simply try saying, "Thank you, I appreciate that." You really do, you know. The compliment just doesn't fit well with your perception of yourself as an inadequate person. Here's an outside voice telling you you're doing well.

While some people compliment insincerely, the majority mean it when they say, "I really like your sweater," or "That was a good report you read at the meeting today." Try not to fight the perceptions others have of you. They might just be accurate. Take the compliment in and try acknowledging it as something another person saw in you that was positive.

Next, challenge the tendency in you to give credit for successes to everything and everyone but you. It's not an act of humility to decline credit for doing something well. In fact, it's a lie. You did speak well at the meeting. You must have done something right as a parent when you watch your kids acting responsibly. You did work hard to get those good grades in school. You did deserve the raise or the promotion. It wasn't just luck. Take back your own credit. Humility means dealing with the truth. And the truth is you deserve credit for the things you do that turn out well. Such affirmation is essential in your efforts to counter depression. You cannot navigate the seas of sadness well if you can't affirm yourself regularly. One of the best ways of doing so is to honestly see and appreciate what you do well that turns out well – and taking the credit.

Principle 5

Learn to value yourself at the level of *being* rather than the level of *doing*.

Much depression results from loss of self-esteem. When you reach conclusions about yourself as inadequate, incompetent and worthless, you have all you need for creating depression. The most common way to lose self-esteem is by failing at something and believing that other people are judging you negatively.

The major mental conversion that needs to take place in overcoming depression has to do with this issue. You need to learn to de-focus from what you *do* and what *others think* as the basis of your self-worth. The source of your self-esteem cannot be your successes and the accolades of other people. Otherwise, you forever remain dependent on the reactions of others to your behavior.

You need to believe that you are not your behaviors. You are not your feelings. You are certainly not other people's judgments of you. Instead, you need to enter inside yourself. There you will find the core of you. At that core you will discover energies or movements toward being a whole and fulfilled person, being a free, self-determining person and being a loving person. It's those movements or energies that make you who you are. And they are good. You are the energies of your heart.

Only when you create a sense of your worth from inside can you overcome the chronic, low-grade depression that weaves through your life. Here I want only to point you in the direction of switching from an outer to inner focus in your quest for self-esteem. How you go about that is beyond the scope of this book. I want to refer you to the **Life Skills Series** book *Accepting Yourself*. In that book I offer you practical steps for turning inward and journeying to the energies of your heart.

Principle 6

Don't let guilt eat you alive.

A form of depression, guilt makes vicious attacks on your sense of self. It's a mixture of depression and anger, insisting that you should have acted or been a different way and then beating you up for not being that way. While it's an important emotion, it hurts you more than it helps you. A little guilt can be productive. It can motivate you to try harder, be better prepared or respond more sensitively in the future. But too much guilt knocks you down and stomps on your sense of self.

In trying to reduce your guilt, it's helpful first to identify the real culprit. Most "guilt" is not moral guilt in any way. For instance, you think the right and correct thing to do is to put money into the collection basket at church. When instead you take a few dollars from the basket rather than putting some in, you may feel guilty afterward. You did wrong. That's moral guilt.

That's not what you usually experience, however, when you say you feel guilty. Usually there is no moral issue at all. You fail to return a phone call. You forget all about the message. When you finally remember it at 11:30 P.M., you feel "guilty." You mention how bad you feel to your husband, who says, "Oh, don't worry about it. Jean said it wasn't important, and if you didn't call tonight to call tomorrow." Your "guilt" is now gone, just like that. Why?

Because you aren't really feeling any moral guilt. You feel bad because you think Jean is now evaluating you negatively. You're afraid she might be thinking, "Gee, Sue is so inconsiderate to not return my phone call." You feel bad because you fear another person is going to be thinking negatively about you. Then you begin thinking bad thoughts about yourself as well. That triggers depression.

To counter guilt, first decide if you're really having a guilt attack. It may just be the sadness you feel over thinking someone is judging you negatively. If that's the case, then you need to fight your self-consciousness. Challenge your thought that the other person is really thinking badly of you. You have no evidence of that. You only fear it *might* be happening. In the example above, once you found out that Jean didn't care if you called tonight or tomorrow, your bad feeling about what she might be thinking of you vanished. If she didn't feel negative toward you, then you don't need to feel negative toward yourself either. The other challenge to your "guilty" thinking lies in realizing you are not the center of Jean's life. She does not spend any more than 10 seconds wondering why you didn't return her call. After that 10 seconds she tells the cat to get off the kitchen counter. You are not the center of anyone else's life. You are not the focus of her thoughts for more than a few seconds at a time. It's not that big a deal!

Another type of guilt occurs when you don't live up to your own expectations. You get angry with your children and yell at them.

Afterwards you feel guilty because you believe you're scarring them for life and because "a good parent doesn't yell." Now, a little guilt here might be helpful. It motivates you to try harder to develop your patience and reduce your anger. But if you take the next step, you're in trouble. You feel guilty about possibly hurting the kids. Fine. But you then start beating up on yourself as an awful parent. Not fine.

Here's where you have to challenge that guilt-ridden thinking. First, normalize your parental reaction. You're believing that no other parent is as awful as you are. You see other parents in the store with their children and they seem so much more patient than you. Hold it right there. Seeing parents in public doesn't count. We all behave with great restraint in that arena. At home, however, all of us get upset with our kids. Most of us yell. Listen to other parents talk, and you'll hear how angry they get with their children at times.

Second, force yourself to not carry your guilt to extremes. Okay, so you yelled. The conclusion is not, "Therefore I am a bad parent." No, the conclusion is, "I yelled because I actually love those kids and want them to learn. I'm a loving parent who yelled." Now perhaps you want to work on not yelling, but having yelled doesn't mean *you* are a bad parent. In other words, try separating your behavior from your being. You are good; your behavior may need some adjusting.

Principle 7

Suicidal thoughts can be reframed as attempts to have a choice.

Thoughts of suicide grow out of depression. They arise at a particular time in the depression. When you feel completely trapped and hopeless, then you think suicide. Why? Because deep within you moves this powerful energy of freedom. You want to be free. You want to be in charge of your own life, feel your own power and have the ability to make choices. You cannot stand being trapped, without any choice at all.

When you find yourself in that state, you will think suicide. You think it not because you want to die but because you want a choice. Trapped in a corner of your life, you have no choice. Thinking suicide gives you – now – a new possibility. You can either stay stuck here in the corner or you can kill yourself. You make the decision to stay in the corner and not kill yourself. And in that moment, you feel a little power. You have some level of freedom. You have made a choice.

If you ever feel suicidal, then, realize it's a signal of a wonderful, powerful energy within you that is still very much alive. You are a free person who wants to live with choices. Once you realize that, you can often discover new and more realistic choices about how to deal with your stuck spot.

Suicidal thoughts don't make you weird or crazy. In fact, they signal the power within you to live freely and in charge of your destiny.

Principle 8

Set short-term, realistic goals.

When you're depressed, you have very little sense of mastery over yourself and your world. Consequently, you rarely have a sense of satisfaction with a job well done. Your emotions and your world have gotten away from you. In that state you want to immediately reassert yourself and begin taking control again. Setting goals that can be accomplished *today* is a great way of stemming the tide of your total sense of helplessness.

The global sense of depression can be overwhelming. It encompasses everything in your life. Once the black glasses go on, all looks bleak and hopeless. It is precisely when you're in this condition that you need to focus on specific behavioral goals that can be acted upon now. Try to draw in your focus and attend to a project or activity in the here and now.

A man whose wife died six months earlier realized he needed to start getting active again. So he decided to paint his basement. He set as his goal to paint the north wall on Saturday. After that his reward would be to hit some golf balls at the driving range. On Sunday he would paint the east wall, then go to a movie. You see, he even reduced the basic goal of "painting his basement" into smaller parts. That way he could feel his accomplishments day by day.

A depressed woman, Kaye, felt her life was spinning out of control. She was in considerable conflict with her parents over the use of the family's summer cottage. She and her husband seemed to be losing intimacy. And she couldn't control her kids. She was yelling at them "constantly," because they were sassing her back about everything. She was also gaining weight faster than ever before. She ground to a halt. Discouraged, depressed, without energy, she literally sat in a chair and rocked.

She needed to *do* something. Her weight actually bothered her more than anything else, at least in terms of feeling out of control. Everything I suggested she had tried, she said, but complained that it didn't work. Her big goal was to lose 50 pounds. It wasn't happening. Losing 50 pounds is an example of a sweeping, general goal. For a depressed person that's way too big. The reward and satisfaction lie too far in the future. Depressed people need a sense of mastery and accomplishment here and now.

As we talked, I tried to help her break the big goal down into small pieces. She ended up deciding not to think about losing 50 pounds but only to drink eight glasses of water a day. She wasn't going to do this to "lose weight," but because it was good for her. Today she could do it and feel good about it. Now, drinking eight glasses of water a day didn't lift her depression, but it did set her on the trail of taking charge of her own life again. That's the value of setting short-term, realistic goals – it gives you a sense of mastery. It counters the depressive belief that you have no control over your own feelings and behaviors.

Because depression causes a sense of helplessness, you want to react with a feeling of empowerment. To gain that sense, you need to:

1. Resist the sense that you have no control over the important aspects of your life. Demand more of yourself, namely, that you have power to take action on your own behalf.
2. Change unrealistic, broad goals to more specific and immediate goals.
3. Decrease the importance of goals that cannot be reached. Often depressed people keep focused on goals they cannot attain. Concentrate only on what is possible for you.

Principle 9

Take action. Make yourself do things that act directly against the depression.

If you need a push here to "get going," go to a rehabilitation hospital and watch people work in physical therapy. John tore up his leg in a motorcycle accident. He had been a very active person, enjoying most sports and outdoor activities. Now his leg was rendered useless. The doctors told him he might never be able to play tennis or basketball again. Sure, maybe he could walk and ride a bike, but he would never again be able to engage in activities that would demand a lot of stress and strain on his leg.

John couldn't accept that. He decided he would do all the activities he had done before. He would work to rehabilitate himself. He never realized how easy it was to say that, but how hard and painful the physical therapy would turn out to be. But he stuck with it. Many days he felt like quitting. The pain penetrated his entire body. The therapists pushed him. He hated them, and he loved them. He became discouraged when his leg didn't respond as fast as he would have liked. But he stuck with it. Daily he struggled. Gradually, his leg began to respond. The little gains he saw pushed him further. Eventually, with a lot of sweat, pain, grit and sheer force, John began walking, then running, then jumping, then hitting a tennis ball, then playing a tennis match and a basketball game, and then went dancing.

He made it because he took action *when he didn't feel like it.* He forced himself to do the necessary things to overcome his predicament. In the very same way, you overcome the killing effect of depression by taking action precisely when you don't feel like taking action. You force yourself to get up and move.

Lethargy grows out of depression like a weed in a moist field. It comes with the territory of depression. Sleep seems more comforting than action. But no. When you become depressed, action is the remedy. To counter the depression directly, you can work in the following areas:

Behavior

Increase all physical activity. Make sure you get exercise. Don't allow yourself to sit and stare, or watch television.

Feelings

Anger often accompanies depression. Try to express your anger in direct and assertive ways. Don't go around yelling at people or harassing them. But speak assertively for what you need.

Sensations

Put yourself in situations where you can experience pleasant sensations at least a couple of times a day. Take a bath, read a book, listen to your favorite music, play golf, do whatever gives you a good feeling.

Imagery

Take 10 minutes a day and imagine yourself acting in successful and positive ways. See yourself taking charge of your life and making decisions for your good.

Thoughts

We talked about this before. Pay attention to those that cause the depression. Then challenge them and replace them with more positive, life-giving thoughts.

Relations

Engage those people who tend to support you, even though you feel you are being a nuisance. They don't feel that way about you. Seek new relationships when possible.

Body

If the depression persists, seek a medical exam. Take extra special care of your body in terms of nutritious eating and exercise.

Principle 10

**Create satisfying rewards when you act
against your depression.**

When you're depressed, you tend to treat yourself pretty harshly. You might not even treat your worst enemy as badly. But then, of course, when you're depressed, you probably are your own worst enemy. Right? Even if you feel you don't deserve any rewards, you need to overcome your mean streak (toward yourself) and give yourself sufficient pats on the back for your efforts to get on top of your depression. You can act against depression by rewarding yourself for the actions you take.

Make your rewards simple and prompt. "If I get up at 7:30 A.M. instead of 9:00 A.M., I can play with my dog for 15 minutes." "If I do my half hour of exercise, I will then read my novel." "If I play with the kids and put them to bed, I will let myself watch Monday Night Football." Some people use monetary rewards, giving themselves money in order to go shopping for a new outfit. Others use food they like. Obviously, with food you need caution so that you don't overeat and then depress yourself more because you have gained weight.

In granting yourself rewards, you may run into the problem of finding that no "rewards" feel satisfying. That's usually a "sour grapes" or "poor me" point in the depression. The rewards that come to mind have always been positives for you. Right now you don't feel you want positives because they interfere with your depression. Here you need to fight the attitude of wanting to stay depressed. I believe that many people "will" themselves into deeper depression. Once they get into it, they choose to stay there. It almost feels good. In a way, the depression becomes its own reward.

When you think of a reward and hear your depressed self veto it, do it anyway. Force yourself to grant the reward for reaching your short-term goal even if the reward seems unsatisfying at the time. When you actually reward yourself, you generally find some gratification. That brief moment of delight helps begin a more positive, upward spiral. Keep on rewarding yourself. Eventually it will begin to feel consistently good.

Principle 11

Act against withdrawing by communicating more with other people.

Depression causes withdrawal; withdrawal causes depression. Again you see the vicious cycle of depression. Forcing yourself to communicate interferes with the downward path of depression. Communication serves as a vehicle for positive feedback. It also carries you past yourself and helps you focus on others. It allows you to see a bigger world, countering the narrow view you take in depression.

Unfortunately, when you're feeling down, you probably don't want to talk with anyone. You want to withdraw and sit in sullen silence, not to be bothered by anyone. Or you might find yourself becoming depressed precisely because you feel alone in your world with no one to share it. Again, the challenge to you at times like this is to force yourself to *interact*. Don't let yourself sit in isolation, moping about your troubled life.

Not only does talking with other people give you direct positive feedback, it yields a more subtle message that you are accepted, cared about and appreciated by others. That helps defeat depression. Such communication tends to improve your self-esteem (the key underlying cause of depression in the first place), and it intrudes into your negative mind set.

Whenever you feel yourself sinking into a down mood, immediately talk with your spouse or your best friend. Creating a communicative relationship is one of the best preventive health measures you can take. A strong, intimate relationship does wonders in helping you remain free from depression. I believe much depression is relational. From teenage years all the way through senior citizenship, depression and the nature of people's relationships go hand in hand. If you have a loving, supportive relationship with one other person, you do much toward avoiding debilitating depression.

Principle 12

To defeat depression when you experience it, you need a specific plan of action in place and ready to use.

I know that when you get depressed, it's easy to feel over-whelmed. Even this short book, written to help you at a time of crisis, might feel overwhelming. It's too much to keep in mind. There are too many principles and tools. You may have forgotten what they all are because you just can't concentrate very well these days. Further-more, you don't feel like doing any of the things suggested. You don't know where to start, what to do first, even though you have just read about a whole bunch of things you can do.

You have to be ready for depression. You have to know your plan of action when you become depressed. So I want to offer you just such a plan. It's based on what you have already read in this section on "Principles and Tools for Defeating Depression."

Simple Plan to Defeat Depression

1. Get a pencil and paper and write down your responses to the items below.
2. Ask yourself: What have I lost that causes this depression?
3. Identify the thoughts you have that cause your depression.
4. Write down challenging thoughts that counteract your depressive thoughts.
5. Set some short-term, realistic goals that you can accomplish within the next day or two.

6. Write down the *actions* you can take right now to get yourself active and fighting against your depression.
7. Write down some *rewards* you can give yourself for taking action and accomplishing your immediate goals.
8. Identify one or two people you can *talk* to, and go do it.

You can do this. I wish I could be there to support and encourage you to fight against your depression. I'm so positive about your ability to defeat your depression because I have seen so many people do just that. I know, you feel as though no one's depression could be as bad as yours. But others who have believed the same as you, have struggled and conquered that heavy mood they carried around for years.

It takes considerable rehabilitation if the depression has nested in you for years. But it can be done. I keep having the picture in my mind of the young man on the motorcycle who crushed his leg. He forced himself, in his pain, to undergo physical therapy. So often he wanted to quit, but he stuck with it, and eventually he again played tennis.

The goal of defeating your depression is satisfaction and delight with yourself and with life itself. Is it worth it? I'm convinced. And I believe that deep within you, you're convinced as well. That's why you read this book. That's why you feel some energy in you to defeat your depression. Work at your plan, and a satisfying, gratifying and enjoyable life will become more and more yours.

Chapter Five

Developing this Skill
with Others

You best defeat depression by working with others. Precisely because depression tends to isolate you, and isolation feeds depression, working with others on this problem serves as a way of countering the depression. You already take a step toward happiness by getting involved with others suffering from the same difficulties.

When you do meet with a friend or a group to learn this skill, you need to make sure you don't spend excessive time complaining about your plight in life. You don't want to feed each others' depression by focusing on it. You want to come together in order to *get out of the depression*. That means you must focus on constructive ways of defeating the depression.

Here's what you can do in a group or dyad setting:

Step One

Spend a limited amount of time sharing what you think you have *lost*. In the initial session, 10 minutes per person should be enough time to identify the losses.

Step Two

Each person writes down privately the beliefs he or she has that create the depression. These then can be shared. Others can help you identify and articulate your beliefs. You want to clearly understand and recognize the beliefs that sabotage your happiness. This could take several sessions depending on the size of the group.

Step Three

Here's the heart of the matter. Take common depressive beliefs that cut across the group and discuss how you can all challenge those beliefs and change them to more positive, life-giving thoughts. Write down these thoughts together and keep going over them on your own throughout the week.

Step Four

When you return the following week, review those positive thoughts and discuss them again so they begin to sound believable.

Step Five

Take a session to set realistic, short-term goals for yourself. Help one another hone and sharpen those goals so they are practical. Write them down, which makes them clearer and more accurate.

Step Six

Discuss action steps you can take. Commit yourself publicly to one another to "do it." For example, "I will go for a fast walk four times this week." "I will take 10 minutes a day to sit quietly and do a relaxation exercise." "I will talk with my wife tonight about our group experience." At your next session report on what you did, what actions you took during the week.

Step Seven

When you create action steps, set up rewards for yourself for the more difficult things you must do or the things you don't like to do. You need support from the group members on this. They may need to help you identify some rewards and encourage you to take them. Again, write them down.

Step Eight

You can make graphs and charts to measure your progress in mood change over time. When you get together, you can record how you feel on a scale from 1 to 10. As time goes on, you will see your progress. Seeing progress reinforces progress and motivates you to keep working at defeating your depression.

Conclusion

The best advice I can give you at the end of this book is simply to **DO IT**. Make yourself take positive action. I know you're on the way toward well-being and happiness because you have already taken the action of reflecting on your depression. That's a great step. Now, keep the momentum going. I know you want to live a full and rich life. Right now you have depression blocking that achievement.

But deep within you, you still have the desire. You're on your way. Stay with it. Don't look back, and don't look too far ahead. Right now you can take action, defeat your depression and enter life fully and positively.

Appendix

Review of Principles
for Defeating Depression

1. Recognize and challenge depressive beliefs in a systematic way.
2. Learn to focus on and appreciate the positive, life-giving aspects of your world.
3. See your successes in *degrees*, not only in the perfect accomplishment.
4. Learn to take credit for your successes.
5. Learn to value yourself at the level of *being* rather than the level of *doing*.
6. Don't let guilt eat you alive.
7. Suicidal thoughts can be reframed as attempts to have a choice.
8. Set short-term, realistic goals.
9. Take action. Make yourself do things that act directly against the depression.

10. Create satisfying rewards when you act against your depression.

11. Act against withdrawing by communicating more with other people.

12. To defeat depression when you experience it, you need a specific plan of action in place and ready to use.